The Ultimate Questions Book ~ Spirituality

Copyright © 2013 Marketing Tao, LLC. All rights reserved. No part of this material shall be used for any purpose other than intended. Nor shall any part of this product or the materials included be reproduced by any means, including electronically stored, without the written permission of Kathy Jo Slusher and Marketing Tao, LLC.

The Ultimate Questions Book ~ Spirituality

Table of Contents

Skillful Questioner 2
Making Questions Powerful 6
How to Use This Book 9
Additional Uses 11
Open and Closed-Ended Questions Chart 14
General Spirituality Questions 15
Spirituality Wheel 51
Life Purpose Questions 52
Relationship to Higher Self Questions 54
Self-Awareness Questions 56
Spiritual Practice Questions 58
Connection with Others Questions 60
Intuition Questions 62
Spiritual Understanding Questions 64
Belief System Questions 66
Spirituality Values / Quality Assessment 68
Blank Wheel 71
Spirituality Quotes 72
SMART Goals Checklist 78
About the Work 79
About the Authors 80
Additional Resources 81

The Ultimate Questions Book ~ Spirituality

The Skillful Questioner

Problems cannot be solved by the same level of thinking that created them.
    ~ Albert Einstein

During the Renaissance there was a massive resurgence of learning and a gradual yet widespread shift in education, leading to economic growth and development, political and social reform, and an increase in trade and commerce.

The Industrial Revolution was a major turning point in human history. There were immense technological advancements, economic progress, income & population growth, and an increase in the standard of living never seen before.

Why?

They were asking themselves powerful questions that shifted the way they approached problems, and spurred curiosity and creativity.

Today, we are on the verge of another major shift. To make the leap we need to make we must ask ourselves and our clients questions that achieve & surpass that same level of curiosity and creativity.

The quality of questions we ask directly influence the knowledge we acquire and the actions we take.

By asking quality, empowering questions we can find the answers leading to the change we seek.

Being a skillful questioner is more than just the words used in the questions. It's as much about how you ask the questions as it is about the words you use. Having no attachment to the outcome of the question and addressing the questioner with curiosity, objectivity and in a non-confrontational manner creates an atmosphere of safety for the questionee to answer honestly and thoroughly.

The Ultimate Questions Book ~ Spirituality

With over 30 years of coaching, training, facilitation, and experiential learning experience between the two of them, both Denny & Kathy Jo recognize even the most skilled professionals can sometimes get stuck finding the right questions.

Asking powerful questions allow the questionee to see things differently, open up creativity, gain new perspectives, see solutions, discover their own answers, deepens relationships and trust, and improves problem-solving and decision-making abilities.

You can ask the most empowering questions and unlock amazing possibilities, but unless you truly listen and the questionee feels that intent, forward movement is stunted. Listening is an important part of communication as is asking powerful questions. However, not all listening is effective listening.

It is said that hearing is a physical ability. We all hear. We don't always listen. Listening is a skill, one that must be practiced and intentional to be effective.

As a vital part of the questioning process, listening enables:
- The acquisition of new information
- Greater insight to the values, strengths, behavior and needs of the questionee
- The questionee to discover his / her own perspectives of the situation
- Trust & Rapport
- Understanding of underlying meaning
- Motivation
- Depth & Intimacy
- Mutual understanding
- The questionee to feel heard and understood

Levels of Listening

There are 4 Levels of Listening. We have all experienced listening to others and being listened to at each level. The higher the level the more energy is required to maintain that level. Not every conversation you have will take place at the Intuitive Listening level.

1. **Competitive Listening**: The main focus in Competitive Listening is on the listener's own thoughts. Here the listener is more interested in their own views and is waiting for an opportunity to jump in and react.

2. **Attentive Listening**: The main focus in Attentive Listening is on the words being said. There is genuine interest in hearing and understanding what is being said but assumes an understanding, not checking with the questionee for confirmation.

3. **Reflective Listening**: The main focus in Reflective Listening is on a deeper and clarified understanding of what is being said. There is genuine interest in listening, not just hearing, as well as understanding what is being said and confirms that understanding, often through mirroring back the exact information shared.

4. **Intuitive Listening**: The main focus in Intuitive Listening is an understanding of the meaning behind what is said. There is genuine desire to understand not only the meaning of what is being said but also the tone, pitch, speed, of what's being said, the body language that accompanies the words, what is being said behind the words, and what is NOT being said.

We all know how important communication is. However, the vast majority of communication isn't spoken. According to studies done in the '70s by Albert Mehrabian, only 7% of communication takes place through exchange of words. The remaining 93% of information is communicated through body language, eye contact, and pitch, speed, tone and volume of the voice.

Understanding that most information is not communicated through words, to be a powerful listener there are several things you have to keep in mind while listening to the questionee.

The Ultimate Questions Book ~ Spirituality

Keys to Powerful Listening

1. Intentions are set to gain a greater understanding of the questionee, their behavior, thinking, values, beliefs, perspectives and needs.
2. Stay Curious.
3. Detached Involvement: the ability to tap into deep levels of empathy and place yourself in the questionees position, understanding their thoughts and feelings without taking on their emotions.
4. Focus on what is being communicated in all areas – body language, tone, pace, pitch, energy – while not focusing on your response.
5. Offer feedback and request clarification if necessary.
6. Remember silence is golden. Don't be afraid of silence. Allow the questionee to sit with the question and ponder.
7. Use Intuitive Listening as much as possible.

When entering a conversation where you are required to deeply listen and understand questionees, try your best to enter the situation with as much energy as possible.

Powerful Questions + Intuitive Listening + Acknowledgement + Time to Respond = Unlocked Potential & Possibilities

Making Questions Powerful

Asking the right questions in the right way is key to achieving the right results. Powerful questions immediately access our creative, holistic brain from which solutions are born. These thought provoking questions are designed to forward your client's actions through clarifying, inspiring, probing, challenging, affirming, exploring, opening new possibilities, connecting, assessing, and evaluating, leading to the right solutions for your client.

When crafting questions, there are 3 things you must consider.
1. The Scope of the Question
2. The Construction of the Question
3. Assumptions & Bias in the Question

Scope

The Scope is defined as the range or subject matter that something deals with or to which it is relevant. The scope covers the domain of inquiry. Matching the scope of the question to meet the needs of inquiry increases the capacity to effect change and sets the questionee up for success. Therefore, keep within realistic boundaries of the situation and questionee's knowledge and power.

For example: "How can you best change your perspective?" as opposed to "How can you change the perspective within the organization?"

When determining the scope of your question you must first determine the scope of the answer you are seeking. If you are looking for greater clarification you must ask questions designed to gain clarity. If you are looking for greater insight, you must ask questions designed to go deeper. If you are looking at obstacles you must ask questions designed to uncover blocks. The scope of the answer determines the category of the question to achieve an appropriate response. You can find the question categories under the General Questions section of this book.

Construction

The construction of a question consists of the language, intention and tone you take when asking the question. A question's construction is a critical element in either opening up one's mind to possibilities or closing the mind to solutions. The construction of a question can determine the depth and direction of the answers. Are you looking for a direct yes or no answer? Ask a closed-ended question. Are you looking for deeper clarification? Do you want to open choices or create a new picture? Ask open-ended questions.

The construction of a question stimulates reflective thinking and deepens the conversation. Starting your question with either "who" or "how" determines the level and direction of inquiry. For example: "Who can help you to make this happen?" "How can this happen?"

When constructing the question, ask yourself what "work" you want this question to do.

Assumptions and Bias

Part of being human is that our experiences and perspectives influence the way we think. We all carry with us assumptions and biases. We cannot eliminate them. Awareness of assumptions and biases allow us to be on the look-out for them as we construct and ask our questions, and listen to the answer.

One of the most commonly used questions containing an assumption or bias is "What is wrong?" This question assumes a negative.

Reframing is a potent way to reword questions freeing them of assumptions and bias such as from "What's wrong?" to "What happened?" Reframing encourages deeper reflection and shifts assumptions into possibilities for creating forward action.

A Word About "Why"

Some of the most powerful questions begin with "Why." Some of the most dangerous questions begin with "Why."

Why-questions can lead to greater insight and more thorough answers. They ask the questionee to go deeper and evaluate. Answers to why-questions speak about the inner feelings, beliefs, and motives of the questionee. Because of the highly personal nature of why-questions safety and trust must be established in the relationship. If not, a why-question can easily trigger reactive behaviors and blame detracting from solutions.

The difference between getting greater insight and triggering reaction is the level of safety the questionee feels in the relationship and the way in which the question is asked.

If safety and trust have been established on both sides of the relationship and a why-question is the most appropriate question to ask, stay curious when asking your question. This will keep the non-verbal elements of asking a question as well as your intention on maintaining safety and trust and away from blame.

Choose why-questions carefully and sparingly.

Characteristics of a Powerful Question

1. Solutions-focused
2. Clear & Simple
3. Involves Values & Ideals
4. Generates Curiosity
5. Stimulates Reflection
6. Thought-Provoking
7. Engages Attention
8. Focused
9. Touches Deeper Meaning
10. Leads to More Questions

How to Use This Book

As you encounter a specific challenge around Spirituality in your life or your client's life, you may become stuck and not know where to go next. This book is designed to assist in getting you and your clients unstuck by sparking new, unique, and in-depth questions. You can either use these questions as is or allow them to inspire new ideas for you.

Open / Closed-Ended Questions Chart: Open-Ended questions are designed to require the answerer to go deeper and give more detail. These types of questions should be used as often as possible to gain greater detail, inquiry, and increase understanding. Closed-Ended questions are excellent for commitment. These are used ONLY when looking for a "yes" or "no" response.

General Spirituality Questions: These general Spirituality-based questions are a great starting point for coaching around Spirituality issues. These questions are designed around a basic coaching approach of: clarifying, creating a vision, defining choice, identifying blocks and barriers, evaluating, prioritizing, probing, and scaling. Use these questions as touchstones throughout the process. Categorized based on your client's specific needs and situation, these questions increase the scope of the coaching relationship.

Spirituality Wheel: The Spirituality Wheel is a self-awareness assessment you can use for yourself or your client to rate the level of satisfaction in each area of Spirituality. You or your client may want to broaden the scope of coaching to encompass each area and be the ideal image of spiritual self.

Wheel Specific Questions: As your coaching relationship deepens and gaps in Spirituality present themselves, you can target different areas of Spirituality more in-depth through these questions. These can even prolong the coaching relationship and develop more spiritual awareness.

Spirituality Value / Qualities Assessment: Rating Spirituality Values / Qualities by how important they are to you and how much you walk your talk can help you identify where gaps may be in your client's Spiritual self. This is an excellent resource in identifying areas and opportunities for growth.

Blank Wheel: When using the Blank Wheel, fill in your or your client's top 8 Spirituality Values / Qualities and rank these to address the gaps of being their ideal image of a Spiritual being. You can also develop new coaching assignments and opportunities around each area.

Spirituality Quotes: This collection of Spirituality Quotes is a great resource for either your own marketing efforts or to deepen the level of thinking for your clients. Use these quotes to send inspirational emails, add to your website, use as topics for your newsletters or to Tweet.

SMART Goals Checklist: SMART Goals help ensure success. Goals that are unattainable or unreasonable are a direct line to failure. Failure stifles excitement, passion, and commitment. To ensure the success of your clients, check each goal against the SMART Goals checklist to determine how viable the goal truly is and keep your client's on track.

The Ultimate Questions Book ~ Spirituality

Additional Uses for This Book

Coaching / Consulting Role

→ Use the Wheel Assessment in a Complementary Session

→ Assess a client's level of satisfaction in the 8 key areas of the Wheel in an introductory session to establish the partnership foundation

→ Use SMART Goals checklist as an evaluation & progression tool

→ Create accountability around the SMART Goals checklist

→ Identify strengths & gaps in each area of the Spirituality Wheel

→ Identify initial coaching goals

→ Use the questions as preparation for coaching sessions

→ Create customized assignments using the questions

→ Create visualizations & meditations based around Wheel segments or Questions

→ Use quotes in sessions to stimulate fresh perspectives

→ Add quotes to client emails for inspiration

→ Create a customized assignment by journaling on quotes

→ Create a mastermind or group discussion around a specific quote

→ Help clients set goals using the SMART Goals checklist

Marketing Tao, LLC

The Ultimate Questions Book ~ Spirituality

Product & Services Development

→ Use this book and the Spirituality Wheel as your Signature Program

→ Use Wheel Assessment in a workshop as an assessment or discussion tool

→ Add Wheel Assessment to your current Signature Program or product

→ Use questions as an idea generator

→ Create an E-course / E-book / E-workbook series around segments of the Wheel

→ Develop workshops & seminars around segments of the Wheel

→ Form Mastermind Groups around key Wheel segments

→ Use Values / Qualities list as an idea generator

→ Write an E-course / E-book / E-workbook on a grouping of values

→ Create Workshops & Seminars on a grouping of values

→ Add a quote to a product or presentation for inspiration or point emphasis

→ Use quote in workshop as a discussion topic

→ Use SMART Goals checklist in a workshop as tool to move participants forward

Marketing Tao, LLC

Marketing / Business Development

→ Use Wheel Assessment as a prospect pre-qualifier

→ Create a prequalifying survey for prospects with questions

→ Use questions or quotes in ezine / newsletter

→ Post a question / quote to your target audience on a LinkedIn Discussion

→ Use a series of questions to outline a promotional teleclass

→ Create a free download of questions around a particular topic

→ Use questions in Blog & Twitter Posts

→ Write an article based on the questions

→ Write an article based on an individual Value

→ Use the Values Assessment as a pre-coaching prep form

→ Create an ezine / newsletter around individual Value

→ Post a quote on your blog / Facebook / LinkedIn asking for comments about how it relates to the topic

→ Use a quote to inspire a podcast or video

→ Use quote to motivate article idea

→ Post Quote on Blog / Twitter

Open-Ended vs. Closed-Ended Questions

Open-Ended questions invite others to discuss in detail what is important to them. They are used to gather information, establish rapport, and increase understanding. These questions do not lead and are not geared towards expected outcomes. When used, the asker must be willing to listen and respond appropriately.

Closed-Ended questions are used to elicit a definitive answer. Use only when you want a definite yes or no. They are particularly useful when gaining a commitment.

Ask Open-Ended questions whenever possible.

Open-Ended Questions Start with:	Closed-Ended Questions Start with:
Who	Is
What	Does
How	Are
Why	Do
When	Will
Where	Can

General Spirituality Questions

Clarifying

Clarifying questions are designed to lay the groundwork and foundation for attaining goals. They set the stage, remove ambiguity, elicit details, and supply known facts.

Ask Clarifying Questions when you need a clear picture of where the questionee is currently at, what resources are available, what perspectives they have, as well as want a picture of where the questionee is coming from, what they want, and the reality of the situation.

Ask these questions as a starting point, to establish a framework.

Example of Clarifying Questions

Questionee: I want to feel more freedom in my life.

Questioner: What do you mean by more freedom?

Questionee: I mean to have the ability to do what I want when I want to.

Questioner: Give me an example.

The Ultimate Questions Book ~ Spirituality

Clarifying Questions

→ Who has made an impact on your life?

→ Who is a part of your spiritual community?

→ Who believes as you do?

→ Who understands your spiritual beliefs best?

→ Who has made an impact on your spiritual life?

→ Who do you admire?

→ Who do you love?

→ Who lifts your spirits when you're down?

→ Who prays with you?

→ For whom do you pray?

→ Who helps you grow spiritually?

→ Who gives you wise counsel?

→ Who inspires you creatively?

→ Who inspires you spiritually?

→ Who makes spirituality accessible for you?

→ Who in your life shares a similar passion as yours?

→ Who wants you to believe as they do?

→ Who shares your beliefs?

→ Who shares your view of the world?

The Ultimate Questions Book ~ Spirituality

→ Who is part of your "spiritual tribe?"

→ What qualities or characteristics make you spiritual?

→ What beliefs do you have around spirituality?

→ What are the qualities and characteristics of someone who is highly spiritual?

→ What beliefs do you have about yourself as a spiritual person?

→ What are your gifts?

→ What are your core values about spirituality?

→ Where in nature do you feel the most at one with God (Higher Power / Universe)?

→ Where does your heart open up?

→ Where does your passion come alive?

→ Where do you want to serve a higher calling?

→ Where in your life are you feeling the most spiritual?

→ From where does your passion come?

→ From where does your compassion come?

→ When does spirituality fail?

→ When does religion fail?

→ When does spirituality succeed?

→ When does religion succeed?

The Ultimate Questions Book ~ Spirituality

- → When do you feel the most connected spiritually?
- → When do you feel the least connected spiritually?
- → Where do you need more spiritual understanding?
- → Where in nature do you like to go alone?
- → Where in nature would you most like to go?
- → Why is spirituality important to you?
- → Why would feeling more connected spiritually make a difference?
- → Why are you searching?
- → Why do you meditate?
- → Why do you pray?
- → Why must you have faith?
- → How do you feel when you are spiritually connected?
- → How do you express your love?
- → How do you express your compassion?
- → How do you express your joyfulness?
- → How would you define spirituality?
- → How would you define religion?
- → How would you define God?
- → How would you define faith?
- → How do you define creativity?

The Ultimate Questions Book ~ Spirituality

- → How would your family describe your spiritual beliefs?
- → How would you describe your family's spiritual beliefs?
- → How do you serve others?
- → How do you share your passion?
- → How do you experience spiritual connectedness?
- → How do you share your gifts with the world?
- → How do you inspire & motivate others?

Visioning

Visioning questions are designed to establish a desired end result. These questions create a picture of the future so a plan on how to get there can be created.

Visioning Questions allow the questionee to "see" the result they are working to achieve. This opens possibilities, engages creativity, and keeps motivation high and direction clear.

Ask Visioning Questions when creating a new reality, establishing an end-result, identifying the ideal, or giving direction to move forward.

Example of Visioning Questions

Questioner: What would you ideally like to see happen?

Questionee: I would like to move to the country away from the noise and congestion of the city. I would like to grow my own food, and live more simply. I would like to see the stars at night and hear the crickets sing.

Questioner: In this ideal vision, what do you see yourself doing?

Questionee: I see myself writing that book I keep talking about and having time to putter around in my flower garden.

Questioner: How would you feel if you had that?

Questionee: I see myself really happy, living a good life with the people I love, enjoying the things that give my life meaning.

Questioner: That is a beautiful picture for you.

Questionee: Yes it is!

The Ultimate Questions Book ~ Spirituality

Visioning Questions

→ Who would you most like to meet? Why?

→ Who would you be if you were completely present?

→ Who would you like to be part of your "spiritual tribe?"

→ What would you do if you knew you could not fail?

→ What would make you feel more spiritually connected?

→ What difference would being more spiritual have in your life?

→ What would you do in life if you were more spiritual?

→ When you become spiritually centered in your life, what will be different?

→ What would you change about your sense of spirituality if you could?

→ What makes you believe you are a spiritual being?

→ What would you do if you knew you could not fail?

→ What does presence mean to you?

→ What does peace mean to you?

→ What would it take to have a deeper connection with your spiritual essence?

→ If you had no spiritual community, what would happen?

The Ultimate Questions Book ~ Spirituality

- → If you were in your advanced years and had an opportunity to tell a youngster the most important thing you learned about living a spiritual life, what would you tell him / her?
- → If you had to describe what spirituality is just three words, what would you say?
- → Where can you go to gain the understanding you desire?
- → How would you like to experience God (Higher Power / Universe)?
- → How could your relationship with God (Higher Power / Universe) bring your energy up?
- → How would you like to be perceived spiritually?
- → How would your life be different without your spiritual connectedness?
- → How would you benefit from going within more often?
- → How would you share your gifts with the world?
- → How can you express your spirituality more fully?
- → How could the world benefit from your spiritual connectedness?
- → How would you like to inspire & motivate others?
- → How is spirituality like a good friend?
- → How could you develop a deeper spiritual life?
- → How would having a deeper spiritual life be rewarding for you?
- → How would having a deeper spiritual life change your life as a whole?

The Ultimate Questions Book ~ Spirituality

Choice

Choice Questions are meant to show options, empower, and accept responsibility. These questions lend to out-of-the-box thinking and demonstrate options and opportunities.

Ask Choice Questions when questionee feels trapped, hopeless, or feels as though there is no other answer, and needs a new perspective & empowerment to move forward.

Example of Choice Questions

Questionee: I don't know what to do. I really would like to attend that seminar next Saturday and Sunday but my husband wants to take the kids to the cabin that same weekend. We always do everything together.

Questioner: If you knew no-one would be upset, what options do you have to resolve this?

Questionee: You mean, if I went to the seminar and my husband took the boys to the cabin without me?

Questioner: What would happen if that could be the reality?

Questionee: Well that certainly would be different. Maybe that would work. I will talk with my husband tonight.

The Ultimate Questions Book ~ Spirituality

Choice Questions

→ Who would you like to model your spirituality style after?

→ Whose decision is that?

→ Who supports this decision?

   → With whom would you like to commune?

   → With whom would you most like to develop a deeper spiritual connection?

   → Who would you become if all choices were open to you?

   → Who do you want to be?

   → What would it take to be more spiritual?

   → What do you like to do with your spiritual community?

→ What would you like to change about your sense of spirituality?

→ If you were coaching someone else in this situation, what questions would you ask them?

→ If you do nothing, what will happen?

→ What choices do you have?

→ What is the toughest choice you have to make right now?

→ Where do you like to go to be alone with God (Higher Power / Universe)?

→ Where is the best place for you to commune with God (Higher Power / Universe)?

→ Where would you like to commune with nature?

→ Where would you like your spirituality to take you?

The Ultimate Questions Book ~ Spirituality

- → Where are your choices taking you?
- → Where do you need God (Higher Power / Universe) more?
- → Where could you use your spiritual connection more powerfully?
- → Where do you want your spirituality to take you?
- → Where do you want to go?
- → When do you need to decide?
- → When do you want to make that spiritual commitment?
- → When are you going to begin that spiritual practice?
- → When were you planning to do that?
- → When can your spiritual choices help you most?
- → When is the best time to connect inwardly?
- → When is the best time to listen to that still small voice?
- → Why do you need to make that change?
- → Why do you feel God (Higher Power / Universe) has let you down?
- → Why would you do that?

The Ultimate Questions Book ~ Spirituality

Blocks & Barriers

These questions are designed to uncover and examine what is stopping the questionee from moving forward, seeing progress, and gaining what they truly want.

Ask Blocks and Barrier Questions when you sense hesitation, resistance, goal hopping, or a belief they are unable to move forward.

Example of Blocks & Barriers Questions

Questionee: I really would like to date again but can't seem to put myself out there.

Questioner: What do you think is getting in the way?

Questionee: I'm not sure…..maybe my fear.

Questioner: Fear of what?

Questionee: Fear of not being attractive enough….of no one being interested in me.

Questioner: So you would rather stay home alone where it is safe than risk getting rejected again.

Questionee: As pitiful as that sounds, yes, I think that is it.

Questioner: How well will that work for you?

Questionee: Not very well at all since I want to meet someone! I guess we have some more work to do!

Questioner: I guess we do!

The Ultimate Questions Book ~ Spirituality

Blocks & Barriers Questions

→ Who gets in your way?

→ Who disapproves of your spiritual choices?

→ Who are you trying to please?

→ To whom do you ultimately answer?

→ Who caused spiritual angst for you as a child?

→ Who is causing spiritual angst for you now?

→ Who would you become if nothing got in your way?

→ Who does God (Higher Power / Universe) want you to be?

→ What holds you back from being more spiritual?

→ What do you hold back?

→ What is lacking in your spiritual life?

→ What blocks your connection with God (Higher Power / Universe)?

→ What is the hardest thing for you to overcome?

→ What is / isn't working?

→ What gets in the way of you experiencing your spiritual essence?

→ What message are you telling yourself that is causing spiritual discord within you?

→ What is in the way?

The Ultimate Questions Book ~ Spirituality

→ Where do you limit yourself spiritually?

→ Where do you set yourself free?

→ Where are you spiritually unsure?

→ Where have you been spiritually fed?

→ Where have you been spiritually depleted?

→ Where is your spiritual connection the strongest?

→ Where is your spiritual connection the weakest?

→ Where are you the most compatible with him / her spiritually?

→ Where are you the least compatible with him / her spiritually?

→ Where have you been the most accepted for your beliefs?

→ Where have you been the least accepted for your beliefs?

→ Where could there be more passion?

→ Where could there be more compassion?

→ Where in your life does creativity flourish?

→ Where in your life do you feel creatively stagnant?

→ When do you need to go within?

→ When do you avoid going within?

→ When are you accepted for who you are?

→ When do you feel the least acceptable?

The Ultimate Questions Book ~ Spirituality

- → When do you feel the most open to love?
- → When do you feel the most closed off?
- → When do you feel safest?
- → When do you feel the most threatened?
- → When are you the most compassionate?
- → When are you the least able to express compassion?
- → Why don't you meditate?
- → Why don't you pray?
- → Why do you feel spiritually empty now?
- → Why can't you live this way anymore?
- → Why change?
- → Why not change?
- → How can you use faith to assist you?
- → How might you be avoiding going within?

- → How much do your thoughts affect your ability to connect spiritually?
- → How can you shift these thoughts to better serve you?
- → How can you shift your beliefs about religion to better serve you?
- → How can you shift your beliefs about spirituality to better serve you?
- → How often to you argue with God (Higher Power / Universe)?
- → How often to you plead with God (Higher Power / Universe)?

The Ultimate Questions Book ~ Spirituality

Evaluating

Evaluating Questions determine criteria. They evaluate or estimate the nature, quality, extent or significance of situations. They assess factors such as needs, issues, processes, performance, and outcomes. They can also determine the cons of a situation.

Ask Evaluating Questions when the questionee needs to establish a clearer sense of their wants and needs related to a particular situation.

Example of Evaluating Questions

Questionee: I want to achieve more success at work.

Questioner: What would that look like?

Questionee: I would work more efficiently and get things done on time.

Questioner: What would be different if you were more efficient?

Questionee: I would lead meetings with more confidence and get more buy-in from the team.

Questioner: How would it feel if you achieved all of that?

Questionee: Great!

The Ultimate Questions Book ~ Spirituality

Evaluating Questions

→ Who do you believe is spiritual?

→ Who do you believe is less than spiritual?

→ Who do you feel the most connected to spiritually?

→ With whom are you the most open spiritually?

→ With whom are you the least open spiritually?

→ Who would most benefit from more spiritual awareness?

→ Whose spiritual beliefs most closely align with yours?

→ For whom do you feel the most compassion?

→ With whom do you feel the most joy?

→ Who offers you spiritual nourishment?

→ Who loves you unconditionally?

→ Who do you love unconditionally?

→ What resources are needed to develop your spiritual practice more fully?

→ What effects do your beliefs have on you?

→ Where have you seen spiritual understanding at its best?

→ Where would you be without God (Higher Power / Universe)?

→ Where could you give more?

→ Where could you be more receptive?

→ Where could you use more spiritual understanding?

The Ultimate Questions Book ~ Spirituality

- → Where could you use more love?
- → Where could you use more understanding?
- → Where could you use more compassion?
- → Where could you find more peace?
- → When, in the past, did you feel the most connected spiritually?
- → When, in the past, did you feel the least connected spiritually?
- → When should a spiritual quest begin?
- → When should a spiritual quest end?
- → When is your energy highest?
- → When is your energy the lowest?
- → When do you feel the most creative?
- → When do you feel the least creative?
- → When does God (Higher Power / Universe) succeed?
- → When does God (Higher Power / Universe) fail?

- → When are you the most committed to your spiritual development?
- → When does your spirituality really come alive?
- → When do you lose sight of your spiritual essence?
- → When is your spiritual connectedness the most enjoyable?
- → When do you feel at one with life?
- → When do you feel isolated and alone?
- → When is your spiritual connection the strongest?

The Ultimate Questions Book ~ Spirituality

→ When is your spiritual connection the weakest?

→ How much spiritual understanding do you possess?

→ How accepting are you of your spiritual nature?

→ How connected do you feel to God (Higher Power / Universe)?

→ How connected do you feel to your childhood religion?

→ How committed are you to your spiritual development?

→ How spiritually aware are you?

→ How much more aware would you like to be?

→ How comfortable are you with mystical experiences?

→ How important is it to have a spiritually-centered life?

→ How connected with nature are you?

→ How much more connection with nature would you like?

→ How strong is your connection with God (Higher Power / Universe)?

→ How clear are you on what you need from God (Higher Power / Universe)?

→ How well do you fit spiritually into your family?

→ How well do you fit religiously into your family?

→ How do you measure your spiritual development?

Marketing Tao, LLC

The Ultimate Questions Book ~ Spirituality

→ How deep are your spiritual convictions?

→ Without them saying a word, how can you tell someone is a spiritual person?

→ How can you tell someone is a religious person?

→ How often do you seek inner guidance?

→ How spiritual are you?

→ How religious are you?

→ How do you know when you have fallen short spiritually?

→ How do you know when you excel?

→ In the grand scheme of things, how important is spirituality really?

The Ultimate Questions Book ~ Spirituality

Goal Setting

Goal Setting Questions are designed to move into and forward the action. They include aspects of accountability, step-by-step action, and an understanding of what needs to be done in order to accomplish the desired goal(s).

Goal Setting Questions are intended to set the questionee up for success. In order to accomplish his there are certain factors to be considered when designing a goal plan.

SMART Goals help construct a format for creating successful goals.

Ask Goal Setting Questions when the questionee is ready to move into action.

Example of Goal Setting Questions

Questionee: I decided I want to return to college and finish my degree.

Questioner: That's great! When would you like to begin?

Questionee: Next semester but I have some things I need to do first.

Questioner: What do you see as the first step to take to get started?

Questionee: Well, I need to talk with an admissions counselor and figure out what credits will transfer and how many credits I need to complete my degree. Then I have to decide which classes to start with.

Questioner: That sounds like a plan. When will you make the appointment?

Questionee: This week. I am excited!
    (Move onto creating SMART Goals *pg 78)

Marketing Tao, LLC

The Ultimate Questions Book ~ Spirituality

Goal Setting Questions

→ Who can help you do that?

→ Who else supports that?

→ Who might get in the way?

→ To what do you want to commit?

→ What is the hesitation about?

→ What do you really want to accomplish?

→ What spiritual accomplishments have you yet to achieve?

→ What do you want to accomplish during this session?

→ What do you want to accomplish in your life?

→ What do you want to experience before your time on earth ends?

→ What can be done about that?

→ What spiritual insights do you seek?

→ Where would you like your relationship with God (Higher Power / Universe) to go?

→ Where would you most like to grow spiritually?

→ Where do you want spirit to guide you?

→ When do you want to accomplish that goal?

→ When is the best time to begin?

→ When have you set spiritual goals before and not followed through?

The Ultimate Questions Book ~ Spirituality

- → When would you know you have succeeded?
- → Why do you want to achieve them?
- → Why change?
- → Why not change?
- → Why is reaching that goal important to you?
- → Why is that goal necessary?
- → Why would you stop yourself from achieving that goal?
- → How would you know you have not succeeded?
- → How would your life change if those goals were achieved?

The Ultimate Questions Book ~ Spirituality

Prioritizing

Prioritizing Questions identifies and weighs importance, values and benefits. They can also be used to rank & order.

Prioritizing Questions are great to use in conjunction with Goal Setting Questions and can also help reduce overwhelm.

Ask Prioritizing Questions when the questionee needs to put their priorities in order or examine what is important to them.

Example of Prioritizing Questions

Questionee: I have so many things I need to get done. I feel overwhelmed!

Questioner: That is understandable considering all you have on your plate. Let's make a list of everything you have to do.

Questionee: OK.

(Together they create a list of to-do's)

Questionee: That's a lot! No wonder I feel overwhelmed.

Questioner: I hear you! Let's chunk it down. Of these 12 items, which are the most urgent and necessary to get done this week?

Questionee: I would have to say numbers 3, 6 and 7. The others can wait. I feel much better.

The Ultimate Questions Book ~ Spirituality

Prioritizing Questions

→ Who do you most want to connect with spiritually?

→ Who would you most like to become part of your inner circle?

→ Who would you become if you made that your top priority?

→ What are your greatest needs right now?

→ What are your top 3 must-haves going forward?

→ What do you think are the top 3 things God (Higher Power / Universe) wants from you?

→ If you could only choose one thing to rely on spiritually, what would that be?

→ What do you need daily to experience the divine?

→ What can you do without?

→ What can't you do without?

→ What is your number one priority with respect to your spiritual practice?

→ What have you dropped that is weighing on you?

→ What is the most important thing you seek?

→ What do you need to let go of to make that your top priority?

→ What do you most want to believe?

→ What old belief do you most want to let go of?

→ Where do you most want God (Higher Power / Universe) to take you?

The Ultimate Questions Book ~ Spirituality

- → Where would you most like to commune with God (Higher Power / Universe)?
- → When is spiritual connectedness most important?
- → When is it important to turn to God (Higher Power / Universe)?
- → When do you need God (Higher Power / Universe) most?
- → When do you most need to rely on that still small voice within?
- → When can your spiritual discipline help you most?
- → Why is that the right choice for you?
- → How important is it to pick that back up?
- → How important is it to find a spiritual community?
- → How important is it to be involved with your spiritual community?

The Ultimate Questions Book ~ Spirituality

Probing

Probing Questions make the questionee go deeper, drawing out more details, concerns, challenges, knowledge, and issues about a particular situation. A good Probing Question requires thought. These questions are used to get out the root of the situation, and reveal thoughts, feelings, and details under the surface.

Ask Probing Questions when going deeper into an issue or concern will bring greater insight and help uncover new awareness; thoughts and feelings lying below the surface.

Example of Probing Questions

Questionee: I really don't want to do my presentation tomorrow.

Questioner: Why not?

Questionee: I don't know. Even though I put a lot of time into preparing it, I guess I don't think it's very good. I'd rather hold off until I can make it better.

Questioner: From what you described last time, it appears you have a solid presentation.

Questionee: Yeah, I guess so. I just think it could be better.

Questioner: Putting the presentation itself aside, what are you really worried about?

Questionee: (Pause) That I will freeze…nothing will come out of my mouth and look like a bumbling fool!

Questioner: That is quite a worry.

Questionee: I didn't realize how anxious I am about speaking to the group.

Questioner: How would it be for us to work on that together?

Questionee: Yes, please! It would be great.

The Ultimate Questions Book ~ Spirituality

Probing Questions

- → Who is God (Higher Power / Universe)?
- → Who in the past used religion to punish you?
- → Who in the past used religion to support you?
- → Who in history would you say was the perfect spiritual leader?
- → For whom is spirituality?
- → Who has taught you the most about spiritual matters?
- → Who has most influenced your idea of God (Higher Power / Universe)?
- → Who did you talk to about God (Higher Power / Universe) growing up?
- → Who do you talk with now about your spiritual beliefs?
- → With whom do you tend to avoid talking about spirituality? Why?
- → Who would you be without your spiritual beliefs?
- → Who do you admire for their spiritual understanding?
- → Whose writings have nourished your soul? Why?
- → Who do you become when you meditate?
- → Who disrupts your inner calm?
- → To whom do you feel the most spiritually connected?
- → Who in your life has taught you how to go within?
- → Who have you told about your mystical experience?

Marketing Tao, LLC

The Ultimate Questions Book ~ Spirituality

→ What mystical experience left you feeling deeply connected with life?

→ What makes you believe in spiritual realities?

→ What does spirituality mean to you?

→ What makes you spiritual?

→ What does spirituality do?

→ What does spirituality look like?

→ What would your life be like without your spiritual beliefs?

→ Where has your spirituality been most appreciated?

→ Where can you be more deeply in tune with your Higher Power?

→ Where can you be of more help to humanity?

→ Where do you find people who share your beliefs?

→ Where can you use your spiritual understanding to make a difference?

→ Where does the world need more spiritual understanding?

→ Where does time stand still?

→ Where would you like to feel more at one with life?

→ Where are you most in touch with your deepest yearnings?

→ Where is the understanding you need?

→ When is spirituality like a straight line?

→ When is spirituality like a curve?

→ When was the last time you offered spiritual guidance to another?

The Ultimate Questions Book ~ Spirituality

→ When was the last time you experienced the divine in nature?

→ When was the first time you had a mystical experience?

→ When was the last time you had a mystical experience?

→ When was the last time you were deeply moved by nature?

→ When was the last time you were deeply moved by God (Higher Power/ Universe)?

→ When have you given yourself over to a higher cause?

→ When do you need God (Higher Power / Universe) the most?

→ When was the last time you asked God (Higher Power / Universe) for help?

→ Why is having a spiritual life important?

→ Why do you seek spiritual understanding?

→ Why is having a deep connection to God (Higher Power / Universe) important?

→ Why does having access to your inner knowing matter to you?

→ Why is he / she happy with your spiritual orientation?

→ Why is he / she unhappy with your spiritual orientation?

→ Why should you accept that belief?

→ Why do you want to accept that belief?

→ Why would someone stop themselves from having faith?

→ Why do you need faith in your life?

Marketing Tao, LLC

The Ultimate Questions Book ~ Spirituality

→ Why are you committed to your spiritual development?

→ Why such devotion?

→ Why would changing your relationship with God (Higher Power / Universe) be important to you?

→ Why do you want to grow spiritually?

→ How would someone know you are deeply connected with God (Higher Power / Universe)?

→ How did you first learn about God (Higher Power / Universe)?

→ How do you blend religion and spirituality?

→ How do you separate religion and spirituality?

→ How much energy do you have around being spiritually connected?

→ How can you feel more connected?

→ How does your spirituality help you?

→ How does the world benefit from your spiritual connectedness?

→ How much more do you want to know about your spiritual essence?

→ How has that spiritual experience changed you?

→ How do power and spirituality relate?

→ How is spirituality learned / experienced?

→ How is spirituality explained?

→ How has living by faith changed you?

The Ultimate Questions Book ~ Spirituality

New Perspectives

New Perspective Questions are designed to shift the direction of thinking. By shifting thinking the questionee can shift the way they approach the world and situations. These questions often create "aha" moments as they elicit options and possibilities previously not considered.

Ask New Perspective Questions when the questionee persists in levels of thinking that include anger, blame, victim, trapped or when they are unable / unwilling to see alternatives.

Example of New Perspective Questions

Questionee: I think my sister is upset with me.

Questioner: What makes you think that?

Questionee: Because she hasn't returned my calls this week.

Questioner: How certain are you she is upset with you?

Questionee: Well, why else wouldn't she call me back?

Questioner: Great question! What might be some other reasons she hasn't called you back yet?

Questionee: Well, maybe she's really busy with work. I know she had a big project she was working on and her boss can set some tough deadlines. I bet that's it.

The Ultimate Questions Book ~ Spirituality

New Perspective Questions

→ Who would you be with deeper spiritual convictions?

→ Who could be your spiritual partner?

→ What might be a different way to think about God (Higher Power / Universe)?

→ If everything was perfect, what would be different?

→ What's compelling you to reach out for spiritual support?

→ What is your deepest spiritual hope?

→ What is "perfect" about your spiritual essence?

→ What is "perfect" about your relationship with God (Higher Power / Universe)?

→ What would make it more "perfect?"

→ What is missing here?

→ What is the one thing you most want to experience?

→ What assumptions are keeping you from trusting God (Higher Power / Universe)?

→ What is stopping you from becoming one with God (Higher Power / Universe)?

→ What do you need to believe about yourself to have the spiritual relationship you desire?

→ If your spiritual essence was a force of nature, what would it be?

→ If you knew without a doubt that you could manifest anything you desire, what would you do right now?

Marketing Tao, LLC

The Ultimate Questions Book ~ Spirituality

- → What is God's (Higher Power's / Universe's) main intention for you?

- → If your relationship with God (Higher Power / Universe) was a story worth telling, what would that story say?

- → If you could go back in time and change one thing about your relationship with God (Higher Power / Universe), what would that be?

- → For what are you most grateful?

    - → What do you most appreciate about God (Higher Power / Universe)?

        - → If the room had eyes and ears, what would it see and hear when you are communing with God (Higher Power / Universe)?

        - → Why would you let that person define your spiritual beliefs?

            - → How far are you from that now?

                - → If you looked through spiritual eyes, how would you see yourself?

            - → How could you look at this situation through spiritual eyes what would be different?

- → How are those assumptions weighing you down?

- → How are those assumptions protecting you?

- → How could you celebrate this new awareness?

- → If you truly believed you were loved unconditionally, how would that change things?

- → How could you show your appreciation more fully?

- → How have you contributed to the success of the Universe?

The Ultimate Questions Book ~ Spirituality

Scaling

Scaling Questions help gauge and determine the level of concern, commitment, and importance. They are a tool that identifies where the questionee would position themselves, the situation or determining a level. Scaling Questions can be used to help measure progress, attitude and behavioral change, and situational shifts.

Ask Scaling Questions when the questionee wants to gauge the level of concern, commitment, or importance of a situation or concern.

Example of Scaling Questions

Questioner: On a scale of 1-10, 1 being not at all and 10 being extremely, how important is that for you?

Questionee: I would say about an 8.5.

Questioner: That's pretty important!

Questionee: Yes, it really it.

Marketing Tao, LLC

Scaling Questions

- On a Scale of 1 to 10 (10 = excellent and 1 = terrible) where would you rank your overall understanding of spiritual matters? Why did you rank yourself that way?

- On a Scale of 1 to 10 (10 = excellent and 1 = terrible) where would you rank your overall Spiritual connectedness? Why did you rank yourself that way?

- On a Scale of 1 to 10 (10 = excellent and 1 = terrible) where would you rank your relationship to your Higher Power? Why did you rank yourself that way?

- On a Scale of 1 to 10 (10 = completely and 1 = not at all) how committed are you to living a Spiritual life? Why did you rank yourself that way?

- On a Scale of 1 to 10 (10 = completely and 1 = none) how much compassion do you carry with you on a daily basis? Why did you rank yourself that way?

- On a Scale of 1 to 10 (10 = completely and 1 = not at all) how spiritually depleted do you feel? Why did you rank yourself that way?

- On a Scale of 1 to 10 (10 = completely and 1 = not at all) how much conviction do you have around your beliefs? Why did you rank yourself that way?

- On a Scale of 1 to 10 (10 = completely and 1 = not at all) how supported to you feel in your spiritual quest?

- On a Scale of 1 to 10 (10 = completely and 1 = not at all) how much do you want to integrate spiritual practices into your daily life?

- On a Scale of 1 to 10 (10 = completely and 1 = not at all) how ready are you to embark on a spiritual quest? Why did you rank yourself that way?

The Ultimate Questions Book ~ Spirituality

Spirituality Wheel

Directions: for each section of the Spirituality Wheel, circle the number that represents your current level of satisfaction in that area. The higher the number, the greater your level of satisfaction.

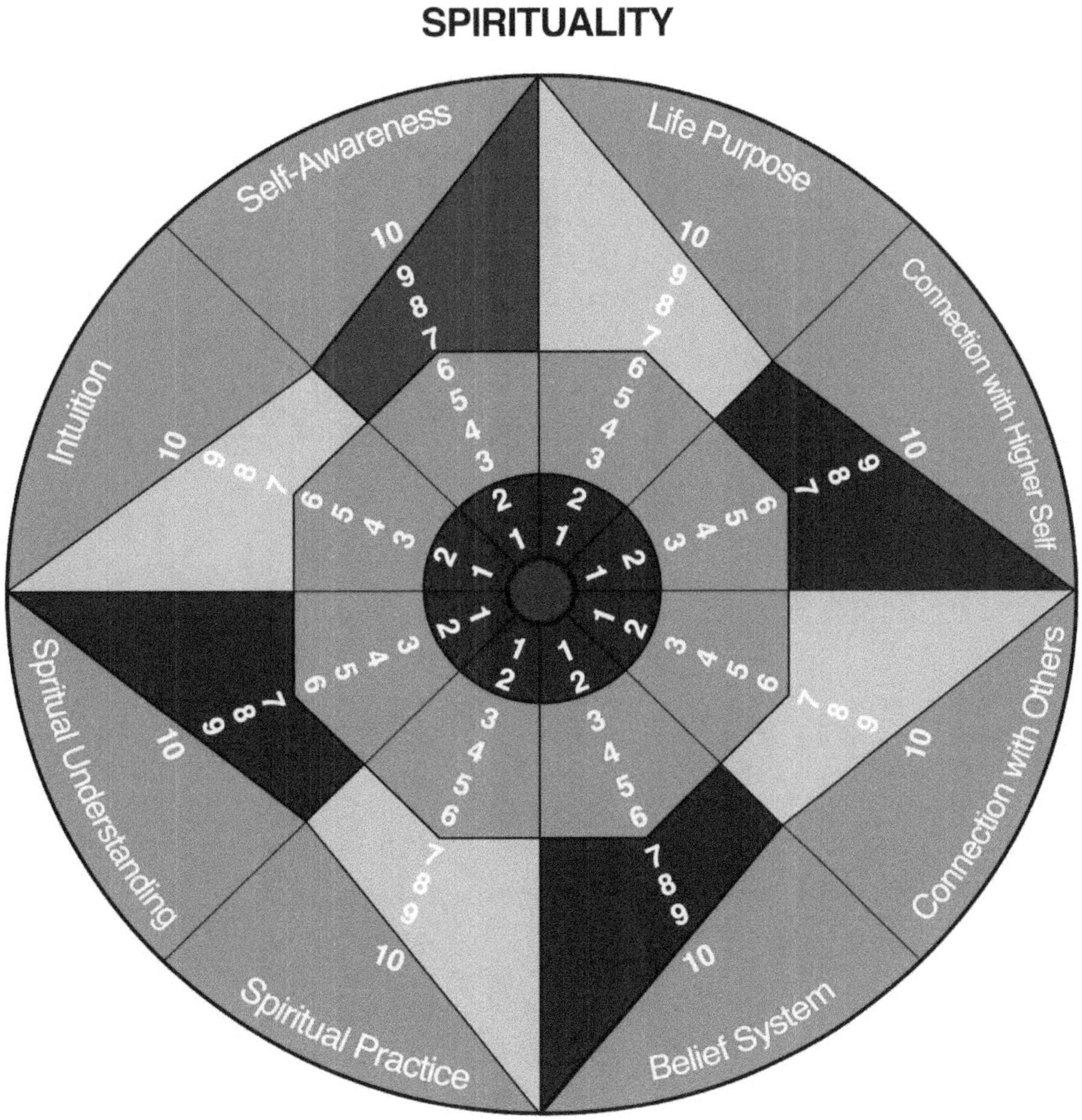

SPIRITUALITY

(Sections: Self-Awareness, Life Purpose, Connection with Higher Self, Connection with Others, Belief System, Spiritual Practice, Spiritual Understanding, Intuition — each scaled 1–10)

© 2013 Unaltered Reproduction Rights Granted, Marketing Tao, LLC

The Ultimate Questions Book ~ Spirituality

Life Purpose

Who

→ Who knows what your life purpose is?

→ Who understands and supports your calling?

→ Who is unsupportive of your calling?

→ Who currently benefits from your calling?

→ Who could benefit more from your calling?

What

→ What does having a life purpose mean to you?

→ What is your life purpose?

→ What does your purpose require of you?

→ What is yours, and yours alone, to do?

→ What legacy would you like to leave behind?

Where

→ Where is your life's purpose taking you?

→ Where would you like your life's purpose to take you?

→ Where do you find the passion for this path you have chosen?

→ Where does one discover purpose in life?

→ Where can you give your life more meaning?

Marketing Tao, LLC

When

→ When are you most engaged with your life's purpose?

→ When are you least engaged?

→ When does your calling and everyday life align beautifully?

→ When does your calling and everyday life conflict?

→ When are you at your very best?

Why

→ Why is having a purpose in life important to you?

→ Why are you uncertain of your life's purpose?

→ Why do you need more clarity?

→ Why have you struggled with defining your life's purpose?

→ Why do people need a purpose in life?

How

→ How can you discover what is yours to do?

→ How often do you feel purposeless?

→ How would you benefit from living a purpose-filled life?

→ How would others benefit?

→ How can you ask for the clarity you need?

Your Questions on Life Purpose

→ _____

→ _____

→ _____

→ _____

Relationship to Higher Self

Who

→ Who taught you how to rise above your limitations?

→ Who is your Highest Self?

→ Who would you be if you lived from your Highest Self always?

→ Who tries to hold you down?

→ Who do you have to be to rise up?

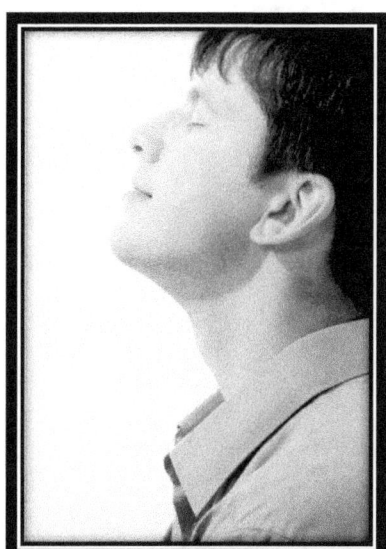

What

→ What is your Higher Self?

→ What enables you to transcend beyond ego?

→ What would you do if you fully relied on your Higher Self?

→ What does your Higher Self have to teach you?

→ What gets in the way of you living from the highest expression of yourself?

Where

→ Where is your Higher Self most present?

→ Where is your ego most present?

→ Where can you quiet your ego more?

→ Where would you be if your higher, wiser self was fully in charge?

→ Where does your ego cause the most mischief?

→ Where does your Higher Self feel its power?

When

→ When do you feel the most transcendent?

→ When do you feel the most dragged down?

→ When would you most like to experience higher states of consciousness?

→ When are you most aware of the presence of God (Higher Power / Universe)?

→ When do you become one with all that is?

Why

→ Why is having a relationship with your Higher Self important to you?

→ Why is transcending the ego difficult?

→ Why does your ego protest?

→ Why are your Higher Self and ego at odds?

→ Why would connecting with your Higher Self in this situation help you?

How

→ How often do you feel you are living from your Highest Self?

→ How often do you feel your ego is running the show?

→ How can you temper your ego to reach greater heights?

→ How can you increase your spiritual power of transcendence?

→ How would that help you?

Your Questions on Relationship to Higher Self

→ _____

→ _____

The Ultimate Questions Book ~ Spirituality

Self-Awareness

Who

→ Who are you really?

→ Who sees the real you?

→ Who do you want to become?

→ Who would benefit most from you reaching your fullest potential? How?

→ Who lives in you?

What

→ What is self-awareness to you?

→ What awareness do you need to grow through this challenge?

→ What are your three greatest strengths?

→ What person do you want to become?

→ What do you need to do to overcome, embrace, or become the person you were meant to be?

Where

→ Where do you feel the most authentic? Why?

→ Where do you feel the least authentic? Why?

→ Where do you need to heal?

→ Where do you need to grow?

→ Where can you get the support you need?

The Ultimate Questions Book ~ Spirituality

When

- → When have you triumphed?
- → When do you know yourself best? Why?
- → When do you know yourself least? Why?
- → When does the world see the real you?
- → When is the real you hidden?

Why

- → Why is honoring your spiritual essence important to you?
- → Why do you want to grow?
- → Why do you find being a spiritual being having a human experience challenging?
- → Why do you want to heal?
- → Why do you want to embrace your truth?

How

- → How could realizing your fullest potential help you?
- → How can you discover your true essence?
- → How can you embrace the real you?
- → How willing are you to let go of all false notions about yourself?
- → How can you begin to do that?

Your Questions on Self-Awareness

- → _____
- → _____
- → _____

The Ultimate Questions Book ~ Spirituality

Spiritual Practice

Who

- → Who supports your spiritual practices?
- → Who doesn't? Why?
- → Who can you turn to for spiritual advice?
- → Who thinks you are frivolous for wanting to meditate (pray, do yoga, etc.) regularly?
- → Who do you have to become to fully embrace regular spiritual practice?

What

- → What do you enjoy most about your spiritual practice?
- → What thoughts come up for you when thinking of spiritual practice or spiritual ritual?
- → What stops you from being more diligent with your practice?
- → In what way(s) are you different when you practice regularly?
- → What would be your ideal spiritual practice?

Where

- → Where are your greatest challenges with your spiritual practice?
- → Where can you shift perspectives about these challenges?
- → Where do you need more spiritual discipline in your life?
- → Where do you participate in spiritual practice?
- → Where might it serve you to be more diligent with your spiritual practice?

Marketing Tao, LLC

When

→ When do you gravitate to your spiritual practice?

→ When do you avoid your spiritual practice?

→ When do you most need to meditate (pray, do yoga, etc)?

→ When do find your discipline fails you?

→ When is the best time to meditate (pray, do yoga, etc)?

Why

→ Why is having a spiritual practice important to you?

→ Why do you like these rituals?

→ Why do you feel better after your spiritual practice?

→ Why is consistent practice hard to achieve?

→ Why have you decided you need a spiritual practice?

How

→ How can you make your spiritual practice more of a priority?

→ How beneficial would that be for you?

→ How could you learn new methods?

→ How much time do you want to commit to your spiritual practice daily / weekly?

→ How many different practices or rituals do you have?

Your Questions on Spiritual Practice

→ _____

→ _____

→ _____

Connection with Others

The Ultimate Questions Book ~ Spirituality

Who

- Who makes up your spiritual community?
- Who in your life would you like to become a part of your community?
- Who supports your spiritual strivings?
- With whom can you talk about spiritual matters?
- Who inspires you to reach greater spiritual heights?

What

- What does spiritual community mean to you?
- What benefits do you derive from your spiritual community?
- To what spiritual community would you like to belong?
- What would your life look like if you had a strong spiritual community?
- What would your life feel like if you didn't have your community?

Where

- Where is your spiritual community?
- Where can you cultivate a spiritual community?
- Where can having a spiritual community help you?
- Where do you get supported spiritually?
- Where do you give spiritual support?

Marketing Tao, LLC

The Ultimate Questions Book ~ Spirituality

When

- → When do you most rely on your spiritual community? Why?
- → When do you feel most connected with your community? Why?
- → When do you feel the least connected? Why?
- → When is community necessary? Why?
- → When have you felt the absolute best about your community?

Why

- → Why is having a spiritual community important to you?
- → Why did you leave your spiritual community?
- → Why did you join this spiritual community?
- → Why haven't you sought a spiritual community (before now)?
- → Why do you need others of like-mind around you?

How

- → How does having a spiritual community benefit you?
- → How would having a spiritual community improve your life?
- → How could you find a group of like-minded people?
- → How would you feel if you had a goodly number of like-minded friends?
- → How engaged are you with your spiritual community?

Your Questions on Connection with Others

- → _____
- → _____
- → _____

The Ultimate Questions Book ~ Spirituality

Intuition

Who

- → Who respects your intuitive wisdom?
- → With whom is the easiest for you to connect intuitively? Why?
- → Who taught you about intuition?
- → Who would you be without your inner guidance system?
- → Who is your intuition cautioning you about right now?

What

- → What does having intuition mean to you?
- → What can you do to develop your intuition?
- → What does intuition sound like? Feel like?
- → What would your life look like if your intuitive guidance wasn't working?
- → What is your intuition alerting you to right now?

Where

- → Where do you find intuition?
- → Where is your intuition the strongest?
- → Where is your intuition the weakest?
- → Where do you need to rely on your intuition more?
- → Where would you be without your intuitive wisdom?

The Ultimate Questions Book ~ Spirituality

When

- → When is your intuition strongest?
- → When is your intuition weakest?
- → When do you most rely on your intuition?
- → When is the best time to trust your gut?
- → When is the best time to listen to your heart?

Why

- → Why does intuition exist?
- → Why is relying on intuition essential?
- → Why do you trust your intuition?
- → Why have you had difficultly trusting your intuition in the past?
- → Why does intuition help you?

How

- → How do you know when your intuition is working?
- → How well do you listen to your gut?
- → How would having a clear and direct channel to your heart be beneficial?
- → How can you learn to trust your intuition more?
- → How can you use intuitive guidance in this situation?

Your Questions on Intuition

- → _____
- → _____
- → _____

Spiritual Understanding

Who

→ Who are you at your core?

→ Who would you be if your spiritual connection was at its best?

→ Who are you when your spiritual connection is severed?

→ Who has given you the spiritual understanding you need?

→ With whom do you need more spiritual connection?

What

→ What does spiritual integration mean to you?

→ What needs to happen for you to feel spiritually connected?

→ What does your soul need?

→ What does your spirit need?

→ What can you do to give your soul / spirit what it needs?

Where

→ Where does your spiritual connectedness tend to break down?

→ Where do you connect with God (Higher Power / Universe)?

→ Where do you disconnect from God (Higher Power / Universe)?

→ Where do you need deeper connection?

→ Where can you find that deep connection?

The Ultimate Questions Book ~ Spirituality

When

- → When is the right time to connect with God (Higher Power / Universe)?
- → When do you shy away from that connection?
- → When is your connection best?
- → When is your connection the worst?
- → When do you feel the most at peace?

Why

- → Why is spirituality essential in your life?
- → Why do you seek spiritual integration?
- → Why has it worked?
- → Why is living a spiritually-integrated life difficult to achieve?
- → Why is walking your spiritual talk essential?

How

- → How does your level of spiritual understanding affect your relationships?
- → How do you know you are walking your spiritual talk?
- → How can you improve your spiritual connectedness?
- → How can you go within and find your wise voice?
- → How would you be different if you felt spiritually connected every day?

Your Questions on Spiritual Understanding

- → _____
- → _____

The Ultimate Questions Book ~ Spirituality

Belief System

Who

→ Who would you be without your spiritual beliefs?

→ Who epitomizes spiritual understanding for you?

→ With whom do you have the most similar beliefs? Why?

→ With whom do you disagree spiritually? Why?

→ Who have you become as a result of your beliefs?

What

→ What does believing mean to you?

→ What is the benefit of having this set of beliefs?

→ What is the downside?

→ What three qualities best describe someone who believes as you do?

→ What are your top 3 most important spiritual beliefs?

Where

→ Where are your beliefs the strongest?

→ Where are your beliefs the weakest?

→ Where do you find people of similar belief?

→ Where would your relationships be without your spiritual understanding?

→ Where in your life could you use your beliefs more effectively?

Marketing Tao, LLC

When

→ When are your beliefs most essential?

→ When have your beliefs been the most challenged?

→ When have your beliefs been the most challenging to actually live?

→ When are you most reliant on your beliefs?

→ When are you the least?

Why

→ Why are your spiritual beliefs important to you?

→ Why is having someone to share your beliefs with important?

→ Why do you believe as you do?

→ Why do those beliefs help you?

→ Why would you share your beliefs with others?

How

→ How would you describe your beliefs?

→ How do your spiritual beliefs help you?

→ How did you come to embrace these beliefs?

→ How can your beliefs be cultivated?

→ How do you communicate your beliefs to others?

Your Questions on Belief System

→ _____

→ _____

→ _____

→ _____

The Ultimate Questions Book ~ Spirituality

Spirituality Values / Qualities

Directions: Identify your top 8 Spirituality Values / Qualities. How closely do you live these Values / Qualities?

- ☐ Abundance
- ☐ Acceptance
- ☐ Affirmation
- ☐ Atonement
- ☐ Authenticity
- ☐ Awareness
- ☐ Balance
- ☐ Beauty
- ☐ Being
- ☐ Blessing
- ☐ Bliss
- ☐ Body Temple
- ☐ Brotherhood
- ☐ Change
- ☐ Cheerfulness
- ☐ Clarity
- ☐ Collective Consciousness
- ☐ Comfort
- ☐ Commitment
- ☐ Communication
- ☐ Community
- ☐ Compassion
- ☐ Communion
- ☐ Concentration
- ☐ Consciousness
- ☐ Connectedness
- ☐ Courage
- ☐ Co-creation
- ☐ Creation
- ☐ Creativity
- ☐ Dedication
- ☐ Delight
- ☐ Desire
- ☐ Detachment
- ☐ Divine
- ☐ Divine Mind
- ☐ Divine Will
- ☐ Devotion
- ☐ Dominion
- ☐ Efficiency
- ☐ Empathy
- ☐ Empowerment
- ☐ Encouragement
- ☐ Endurance
- ☐ Energy
- ☐ Eternal Life
- ☐ Enthusiasm
- ☐ Evolution
- ☐ Expectancy
- ☐ Expression
- ☐ Faith
- ☐ Family
- ☐ Flexibility
- ☐ Forgiveness
- ☐ Freedom
- ☐ Free Will

© 2013 Unaltered Reproduction Rights Granted, Marketing Tao, LLC

The Ultimate Questions Book ~ Spirituality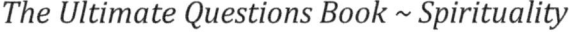

- ☐ Fulfillment
- ☐ Generosity
- ☐ Giving
- ☐ God
- ☐ Grace
- ☐ Gratitude
- ☐ Growth
- ☐ Guidance
- ☐ Harmony
- ☐ Healing
- ☐ Health
- ☐ Holiness
- ☐ Hope
- ☐ Honesty
- ☐ Higher Power
- ☐ Humankind
- ☐ Humility
- ☐ Illumination
- ☐ Imagination
- ☐ Immanence
- ☐ Inspiration
- ☐ Integrity
- ☐ Interconnectedness
- ☐ Intention
- ☐ Intuition
- ☐ Joy
- ☐ Judgment
- ☐ Karma
- ☐ Law
- ☐ Legacy
- ☐ Letting Go
- ☐ Life
- ☐ Light
- ☐ Love
- ☐ Manifestation
- ☐ Meditation
- ☐ Mind
- ☐ Mindfulness
- ☐ Miracle
- ☐ Motivation
- ☐ Mutual Support
- ☐ Mystery
- ☐ Mercy
- ☐ Non-judgment
- ☐ Non-resistance
- ☐ Obedience
- ☐ Oneness
- ☐ Open Heart
- ☐ Openness
- ☐ Order
- ☐ Other
- ☐ Passion
- ☐ Patience
- ☐ Peacefulness
- ☐ Playfulness
- ☐ Potentiality
- ☐ Power
- ☐ Praise
- ☐ Prayer
- ☐ Presence
- ☐ Principle
- ☐ Prosperous
- ☐ Protective
- ☐ Purification

© 2013 Unaltered Reproduction Rights Granted, Marketing Tao, LLC

The Ultimate Questions Book ~ Spirituality

- ☐ Purpose
- ☐ Purity
- ☐ Rebirth
- ☐ Receiving
- ☐ Renunciation
- ☐ Realization
- ☐ Reincarnation
- ☐ Regeneration
- ☐ Relaxation
- ☐ Release
- ☐ Repentance
- ☐ Resurrection
- ☐ Reverence
- ☐ Sabbath
- ☐ Salvation
- ☐ Security
- ☐ Seeing the Good
- ☐ Self-Awareness
- ☐ Self-Knowledge
- ☐ Self-Realization
- ☐ Selflessness
- ☐ Service
- ☐ Silence
- ☐ Simplicity
- ☐ Sisterhood
- ☐ Spirit
- ☐ Spirituality
- ☐ Soul
- ☐ Source
- ☐ Spontaneity
- ☐ Steadfastness
- ☐ Stewardship

- ☐ Stillness
- ☐ Strength
- ☐ Substance
- ☐ Support
- ☐ Surrender
- ☐ Synergy
- ☐ Sincerity
- ☐ Synthesis
- ☐ Tenderness
- ☐ Thankfulness
- ☐ Thoughtfulness
- ☐ Tolerance
- ☐ Transcendence
- ☐ Transformation
- ☐ Trust
- ☐ Truth
- ☐ Understanding
- ☐ Unity
- ☐ Unchanging
- ☐ Universal Power
- ☐ Value
- ☐ Visualization
- ☐ Wholeness
- ☐ Will
- ☐ Wisdom
- ☐ _____
- ☐ _____
- ☐ _____
- ☐ _____
- ☐ _____
- ☐ _____
- ☐ _____

© 2013 Unaltered Reproduction Rights Granted, Marketing Tao, LLC

Blank Spirituality Wheel

The Ultimate Questions Book ~ Spirituality

Directions: In the blank sections of the wheel add your top 8 Spirituality Values / Qualities from the previous assessment. For each section, circle the number that represents your current level of satisfaction in that area. The higher the number the greater your level of satisfaction.

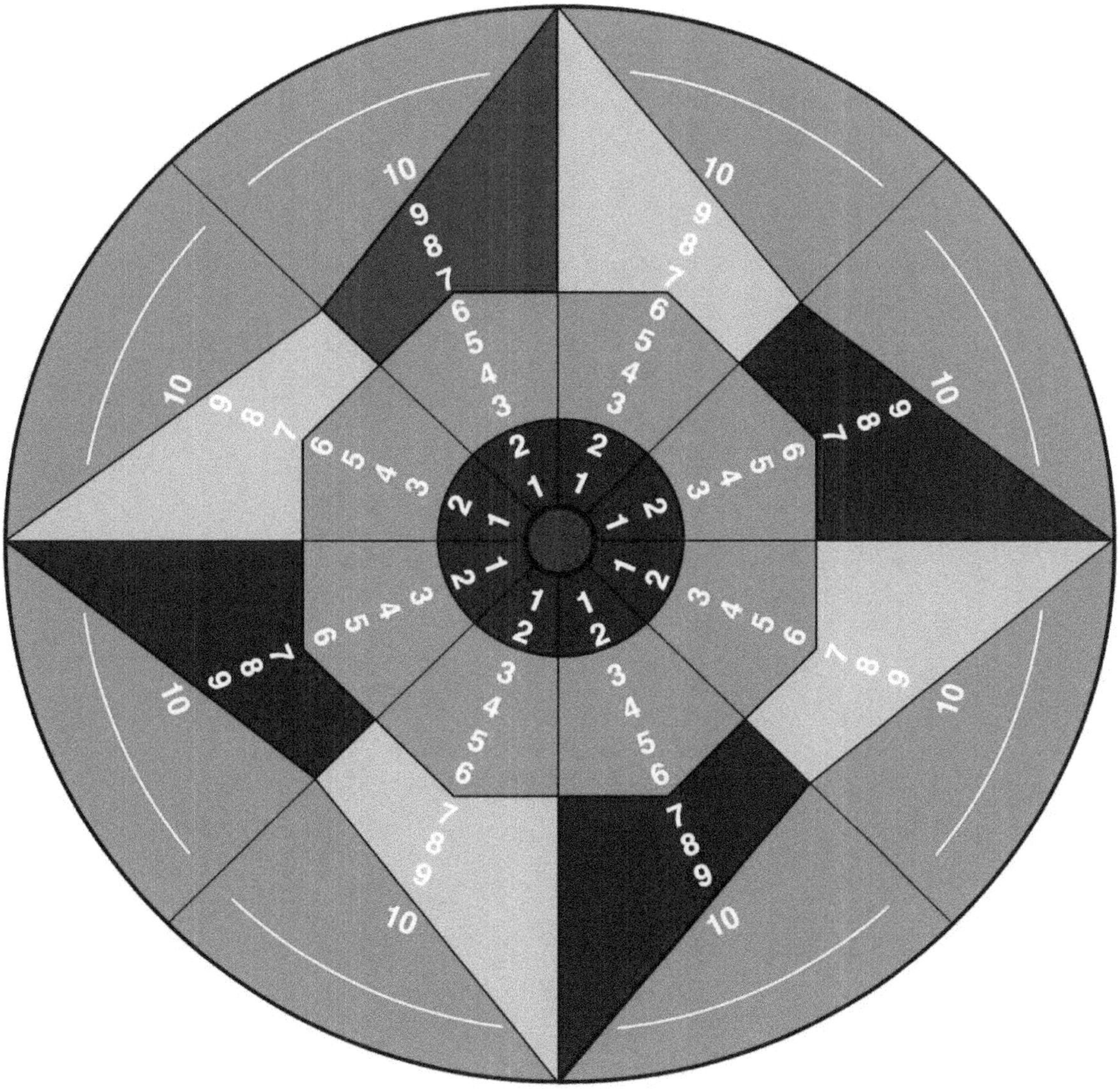

© 2013 Unaltered Reproduction Rights Granted, Marketing Tao, LLC

Spirituality Quotes

My soul remembers.
   ~ Richard Billings

Enlightenment for a wave is the moment the wave realizes that it is water. At that moment, all fear of death disappears.
   ~ Thich Nhat Hanh

Divine Law dictates that every development is initiated by the mind.
   ~ Sonia Choquette

The higher goal of spiritual living is not to amass a wealth of information, but to face sacred moments.
   ~ Abraham Heschel

I have been born again, and again, and each time I have found something to love.
   ~ Gordon Parks

A fish cannot drown in water; a bird does not fall in air. Each creature God made must live in its own true nature.
   ~ Mechthild of Magdeburg

Forget about enlightenment. Sit down wherever you are and listen to the wind singing in your veins.
   ~ John Welwood

The Ultimate Questions Book ~ Spirituality

May the Force be with you.
    ~ Obi-Wan Kenobi, Star Wars

Be ye lamps unto yourselves.
    ~ The Buddha

Wherever you go, there you are.
    ~ Jon Kabat-Zinn

Your Inner Intelligence is also your power source.
    ~ Sonia Choquette

Of magic doors there is this, you do not see them even as you are passing through.
    ~ Anon

Be serene in the oneness of things and erroneous views will disappear by themselves.
    ~ Seng-Ts' An

Perhaps the shortest and most powerful prayer in human language is "help."
    ~ Father Thomas Keating

Who sees all beings in his own Self and his own Self in all beings, loses all fear.
    ~ The Isa Upanishad

Enlightenment doesn't care how you get there.
    ~ Thaddeus Golas

Divine Spirit hides from nothing and judges nothing.
    ~ Sonia Choquette

We are here to live out loud.
    ~ Balzac

Marketing Tao

Man receives only that which he gives.
    ~ Florence Scovel Shinn

Those who go against the grain of God's laws shouldn't complain when they get splinters.
    ~ Unknown

We are all made of star stuff.
    ~ Carl Sagan

If you truly hold a stone, you can feel the mountain it came with.
    ~ Mark Nepo

Just trust yourself and you will know how to live.
    ~ Goethe

Who cares if you're enlightened forever? Can you just get it in this moment, now?
    ~ Byron Katie

It is only by grounding our awareness in the living sensation of our bodies that the "I Am," our real presence, can awaken.
    ~ G.I. Gurdjieff

Bring into play the almighty power within you, so that on the stage of life you can fulfill your high destined role.
    ~ ParamanansaYogananada

Our essential nature is one of pure potentiality.
    ~ Deepak Chopra

The Ultimate Questions Book ~ Spirituality

There is only one reason to do anything: as a statement to the universe of Who You Are.
~ Neale Donald Walsch

At any moment, you have a choice, that either leads you closer to your spirit or further away from it.
~ Thich Nhat Hanh

Man's main task in life is to give birth to himself.
~ Erich Fromm

The coming to consciousness is not a discovery of some new thing; it is a long and painful return to that which has always been.
~ Helen Luke

It is not well for man to pray cream and live skim-milk.
~ Henry Ward Beecher

This is my simple religion. There is no need for temples; no need for complicated philosophy. Our own brain, our own heart is our temple; the philosophy is kindness.
~ Dalai Lama

We love what we attend.
~ Mwalimu Imara

The more spacious and larger our fundamental nature, the more bearable the pain in living.
~ Wayne Muller

Enlightenment must come little by little - otherwise it would overwhelm.
~ Idries Shah

The Ultimate Questions Book ~ Spirituality

Another name for God is "Surprise."
  ~ Brother David Steindl-Rast

The world when seen through a little child's eyes greatly resembles paradise.
  ~ Unknown

You cannot transcend what you do not know. To go beyond yourself, you must know yourself.
  ~ Sri Nisargadatta Maharaj

Live deep enough and there is only one direction.
  ~ Mark Nepo

Everything you see happening is the consequence of that which you are.
  ~ David R. Hawkins

We are not human beings on a spiritual journey. We are spiritual beings on a human journey.
  ~ Stephen Covey

Throughout all the ten regions of the Universe, there is no place where the Source is not.
  ~ Hakuin

We cannot be present and run our story-line at the same time.
  ~ Pema Chodron

Pain is inevitable. Suffering is optional.
  ~ Dalai Lama

Any path is only a path, and there is no affront to oneself or to others, in dropping it if that is what your heart tells you.
  ~ Carlos Castaneda

Marketing Tao

The Ultimate Questions Book ~ Spirituality

If you realized how powerful your thoughts are, you would never think a negative thought.
~ Peace Pilgrim

There are only two ways to live your life. One is as though nothing is a miracle. The other is as though everything is a miracle.
~ Albert Einstein

There are no accidents... there is only some purpose that we haven't yet understood.
~ Deepak Chopra

Life can only take place in the present moment. If we lose the present moment, we lose life.
~ Buddha

The oak sleeps in the acorn; the bird waits in the egg; and in the highest vision of the soul a waking angel stirs.
~ James Allen

We turn to God for help when our foundations are shaking, only to learn that it is God who is shaking them.
~ Unknown

Heaven on Earth is a choice you must make, not a place you must find.
~ Wayne Dyer

The Ultimate Questions Book ~ Spirituality

S.M.A.R.T. Goals Checklist

Specific
- ☐ What precisely is expected?
- ☐ Be as specific as possible.
- ☐ What will you have when the specific task is complete?
- ☐ What will the outcome be?

Measurable
- ☐ How would you know you have achieved success?
- ☐ How many tasks do you need to do?
- ☐ For how long?
- ☐ Make it a tangible process.

Achievable
- ☐ Is this achievable?
- ☐ What would be achievable?
- ☐ Do you have the skills or resources necessary to meet this goal?

Reasonable
- ☐ Is this a reasonable goal?
- ☐ What might be the obstacles?
- ☐ Considering everything else you have going on, can you achieve this goal?

Time-Oriented
- ☐ When will you be done?
- ☐ When will your tasks be scheduled?
- ☐ How long will it take to accomplish each task?
- ☐ When is the ideal time for this goal to be completed?

© 2013 Unaltered Reproduction Rights Granted, Marketing Tao, LLC

About the Work

The Ultimate Questions Book ~ Spirituality

We live in a time of great change. Faced with some of the most difficult challenges our world has ever known, we feel an urgency to find solutions to make our lives better. We want answers and we want them now!

In general, we focus on **getting the right answer not on asking the right questions.** Why is this? Perhaps it stems from an innate curiosity and a desire to make sense of the world. Perhaps it comes from a fear of the unknown or the need for a quick fix. It may also result from the need for blind acceptance of some *truth* where any form of questioning is strongly discouraged or denied. Perhaps we think we already have the answer, so why ask any questions at all? Whatever the case, there is no doubt human beings like answers.

When we focus on "getting the right answers," rather than "asking the right questions," we limit ourselves. We move into dualistic thinking: "I either have the right answer or I don't." We think in terms of yes or no, right or wrong, good or bad. **This black and white framework enables only surface inquiry**, at best, and quells deeper investigation and the ability to engage with others in meaningful ways. We lose the opportunity to generate new solutions to old problems.

Why are asking the right questions important? Because they generate beneficial lasting change. Empowering questions make possible diverse perspectives, which in turn lead to sustainable solutions to complicated challenges. They enable people to engage in dynamic transformational conversations out of which new ideas are born.

To generate the type of change our world needs, **we must raise penetrative questions to challenge current assumptions**; assumptions that keep us disempowered to affect change. The key in creating a positive, empowering future is asking positive, empowering questions now! So, what are you waiting for?

Marketing Tao

The Ultimate Questions Book ~ Spirituality

About the Authors

Kathy Jo Slusher, PCC, ELI-MP, Founder of Marketing Tao, LLC, has dedicated her life to help service-based socially conscious business owners make their business a success through sharing their passion. She believes that when your intention is on your passion and helping others, money is a natural bi-product. *It's not what you sell but what you stand for that makes you a success.* She is deeply committed to helping soloprofessionals and small business owners implement mindful marketing techniques and strategies to attract their ideal clients while making a difference in the world.

Kathy Jo is a Co-Founder of The REAL Results Coaching Exchange, partner in Coaching Skills for Leaders, a member of the International Coach Federation, and Vice-President of the United Nations Association of the US, Indianapolis Chapter.

Denny Balish, PCC, ELI-MP, Professional Certified Coach and Founder of ThreeFold Life Coaching, has dedicated her life's work to the development of Human Potential. She believes that each person has within themselves the desire and ability to be a positive force for change in the world and, by sharing one's unique gifts and talents with others, global change is possible. Denny is deeply committed to helping people and organizations get and stay powerfully on-purpose so they can be the change they wish to see in the world. Denny is a member of the International Coach Federation (ICF), Association for Global New Thought (AGNT), and founding board member of Spirit's Light Foundation, an alternative youth and family ministry with the Association of Unity Churches International.

Other Valuable Resources

For Coaches, Consultants, and Service-Based Small Businesses

 **Ultimate Questions Books**

The real power in transformation is not in the answers, but in the questions we ask. If coaches, therapists or consultants are unsure of the questions to ask, client results are greatly impacted.

This series of books is specifically designed for coaches, consultants, therapists and others who are in a place where they need some fresh ideas to get themselves, a client, or anyone else unstuck. www.UltimateQuestionsBook.com

 **Marketing Made Practical**

Marketing Made Practical is a Home Study Program designed for those who are overwhelmed with all the options and don't have a handle on how to make the marketing process into an effective, successful strategy.

Marketing Made Practical is specifically designed for service-based soloprofessionals or small business owners who are just getting started or have a limited experience and need an organized approach to marketing. www.MarketingMadePractical.com

 **Marketing Strategies University**

Marketing Strategies University is an online training program that walks you through how to create a strong marketing and business development plan.

Marketing Strategies University cuts to the chase of marketing. We don't dive into the theory of marketing – but focus on practical steps to create and implement powerful marketing strategies.

This unique online training program is designed for service-based soloprofessionals or small business owners who have reached a certain level in their business where they are ready to create the systems and strategies for their marketing to take them to the next level of success. www.MarketingStrategiesUniversity.com

Marketing Strategies Success

Marketing Strategies Success is an online membership forum which brings together motivation and information into a community of like-minded business owners all working to create change through their business.

Through topic specific open Q & A calls & recordings, to an interactive forum where members share ideas, to a mentoring component of Success Stories, where successful entrepreneurs share their success secrets, this group will help those who have a message to share through their business but need marketing know-how & structure to accomplish their mission. www.MarketingStrategiesSuccess.com

For Leadership Development Support

Coaching Skills for Leaders

Employees don't leave companies, they leave managers.

According to the Gallup Poll, 71% of employees studied said they were either not engaged or actively disengaged at work. This employee disengagement results in $370 Billion lost annually. That's a huge amount.

In today's environment, talented individuals are arguably an organization's most valuable resource. Yet studies show, high potential employees have a higher turnover rate than any other employee population.

Leaders need to be flexible, adaptable, creative and resourceful to deal with the reality of our economic times. Coaching Skills for Leaders will take

you and your organization through The Coaching Clinic, a specialized training program where you acquire a new approach to old issues. This process offers a step-by-step process of a coaching conversation in how to conduct & lead those difficult conversations. You will learn how to address organizational challenges through a step-by-step structured approach to facilitate your own coaching conversation, and develop partners and accountability standards across the board. Thus you will be transforming managers into true Leaders. www.Coaching-Skills-for-Leaders.com

 ## Lifestyle, Leadership, Legacy

What are you working for?

As a business owner or executive you've worked hard to get where you are at. But how has this helped the lifestyle you want to lead? If you're tired to living to work instead of working to live, this program is for you.

We will identify your desired lifestyle, look at how to improve your leadership ability so you can more effectively lead those around you as well as your own life and create a lasting legacy to leave behind.

 ## On-Purpose Leadership Development

For on-purpose professionals who want to develop their leadership acumen while expanding their consciousness. This program formulates a plan of action to break through all obstacles limiting your success, while building powerful skills to help you lead with purpose, including: manage conflict and chaos with greater ease, use your intuition for effortless decision-making, communicate effectively and persuasively, maximize your ability to engage and influence people in positive ways, and feel empowered to affect change in yourself and others.

For Specialized Support for Non-Profits, Social Enterprises and Cultural Creatives

 ### Life Purpose Coaching

Empowering individuals in their midlife years to create a life of deeper meaning and purpose by not only connecting with their authentic voice and innate wisdom, but also by helping them aligning their skills, talents and interests with their desire to give back in meaningful ways.

 ### On-Purpose Career Transition

For individuals in all phases of career and job transition who seek to purposefully align their skills and abilities with their passion for a satisfying career; one that enables them to give back in meaningful ways. Make a living while making a difference! This program is customized to fit individual needs.

For More Information Contact:

Marketing Tao, LLC
Kathy Jo Slusher
Email   info@MarketingTao.com
Call   317.536.5544
Click   www.MarketingTao.com
Click   www.TheREALResultsCoachingExchange.com

Threefold Life
Denny Balish
Email   info@threefoldlife.com
Call   708.209.6977
Click   www.Threefoldlife.com

www.ingramcontent.com/pod-product-compliance
Lightning Source LLC
Chambersburg PA
CBHW081217230426
43666CB00015B/2768